Engineering and Construction That We Can Still See Today

Ancient History Rome
Children's Ancient History

BABY PROFESSOR

EDUCATION KIDS

Speedy Publishing LLC

40 E. Main St. #1156

Newark, DE 19711

www.speedypublishing.com

Copyright 2017

In this book, we're going to cover the engineering and construction work done by the Ancient Romans. So, let's get right to it.

The Ancient Romans had advanced skills in engineering, architecture, and construction. It's been thousands of years since some of these marvels of construction were built and many still have significant pieces that are standing despite earthquakes and other natural disasters.

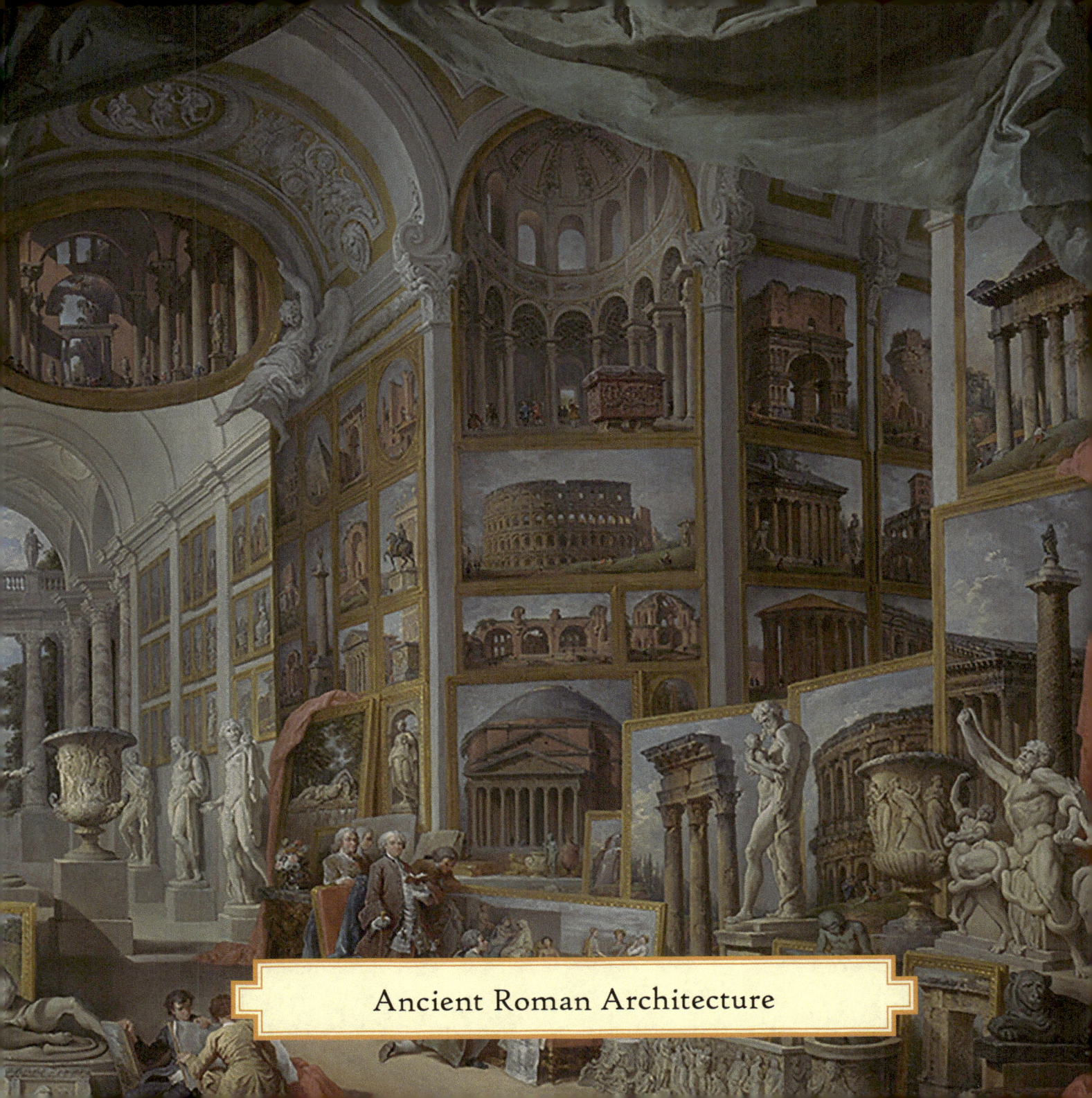

Ancient Roman Architecture

Before the Romans, many cultures including the Egyptians and Greeks had grand architecture, but their buildings were more beautiful from the outside than from the inside. Ancient Romans changed architecture forever. Their buildings were just as grand on the inside as the outside.

THE ROMANS USED CEMENT AND CONCRETE

One of the reasons that so many Ancient Roman structures are still standing today is because they used forms of both cement and concrete. They first began to construct using concrete over 2000 years ago and they used it in everything they built—roads, monuments, aqueducts, bridges, and buildings.

Ancient Roman Structures

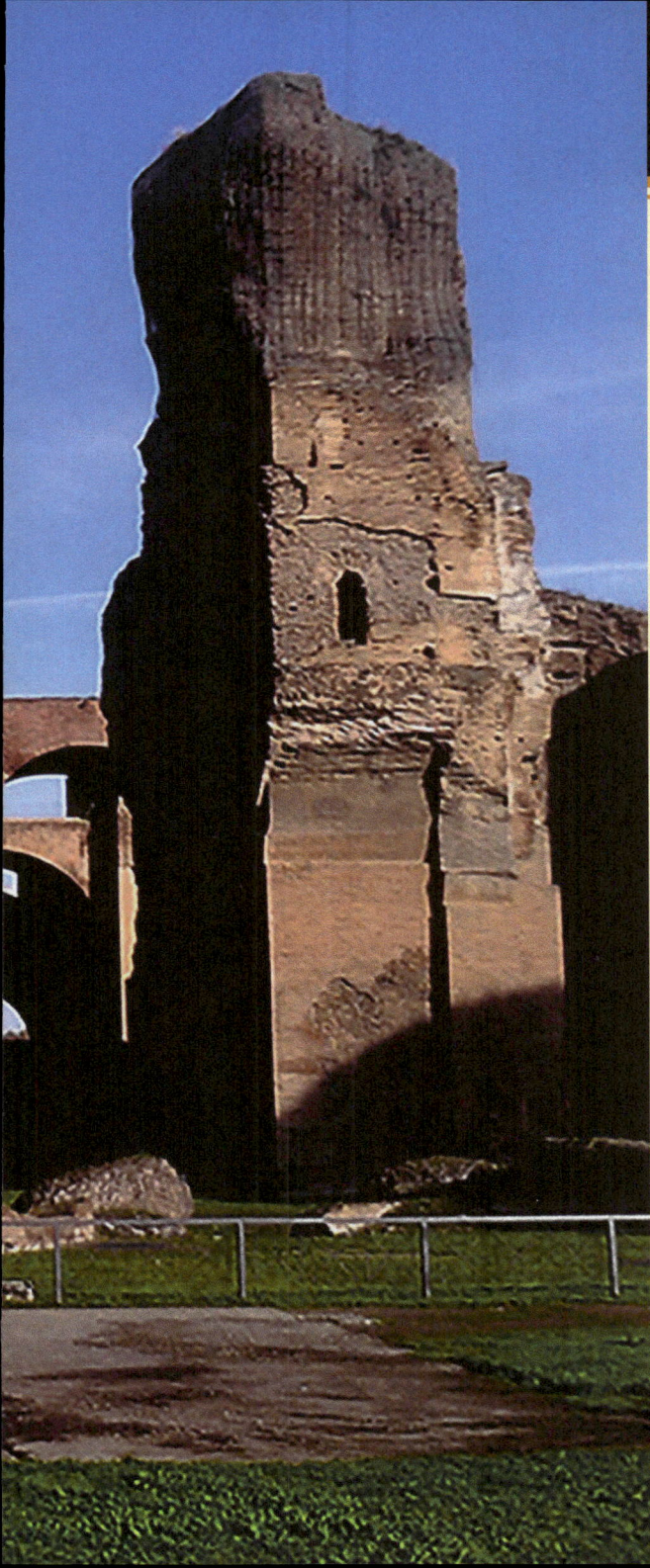

It's true that the concrete the Romans had was weaker than today's concrete we use in modern buildings. They used slaked lime combined with a substance called pozzolana, which was a type of volcanic ash, to make a sticky paste.

They combined this mixture with other volcanic rocks to make a durable form of concrete. Their concrete set quickly even when it was underwater. This made it possible for them to create piers, harbors, and elaborate baths.

THE CLASSIC ROMAN ARCH

Even though arches as an architectural design have been around for over 4,000 years, it was the Ancient Romans who perfected its use for many different types of buildings. By using arches, they were able to build buildings that would stand instead of collapsing from the weight of the stones used to build them.

They improved the design of arches by flattening their shape, creating what is called a segmental arch. Then, they repeated these arches at regular points to construct stronger supports that could span the types of gaps needed for aqueducts and bridges.

DEFINING FEATURES OF ANCIENT ROMAN ARCHITECTURE

As you study the different Ancient Roman structures that are still standing, you'll notice some common features. Many have elaborate arches, sometimes built on top of each other and joined together columns. In many ways they were adapted from the columns used by the Ancient Greeks domes, such as the one at the Pantheon, which allowed them to build wide open interior spaces inside their buildings with vaulted ceilings, which were arrangements of arches to form roofs

THE COLOSSEUM

The Colosseum in the city of Rome is a prime example of the skills the Ancient Romans had as engineers and architects. Construction began in 72 AD and was completed eight years later. This gigantic elliptical outdoor amphitheater held 50,000 people for the bloody sports and entertainment of the day, such as gladiator combat and animal hunts.

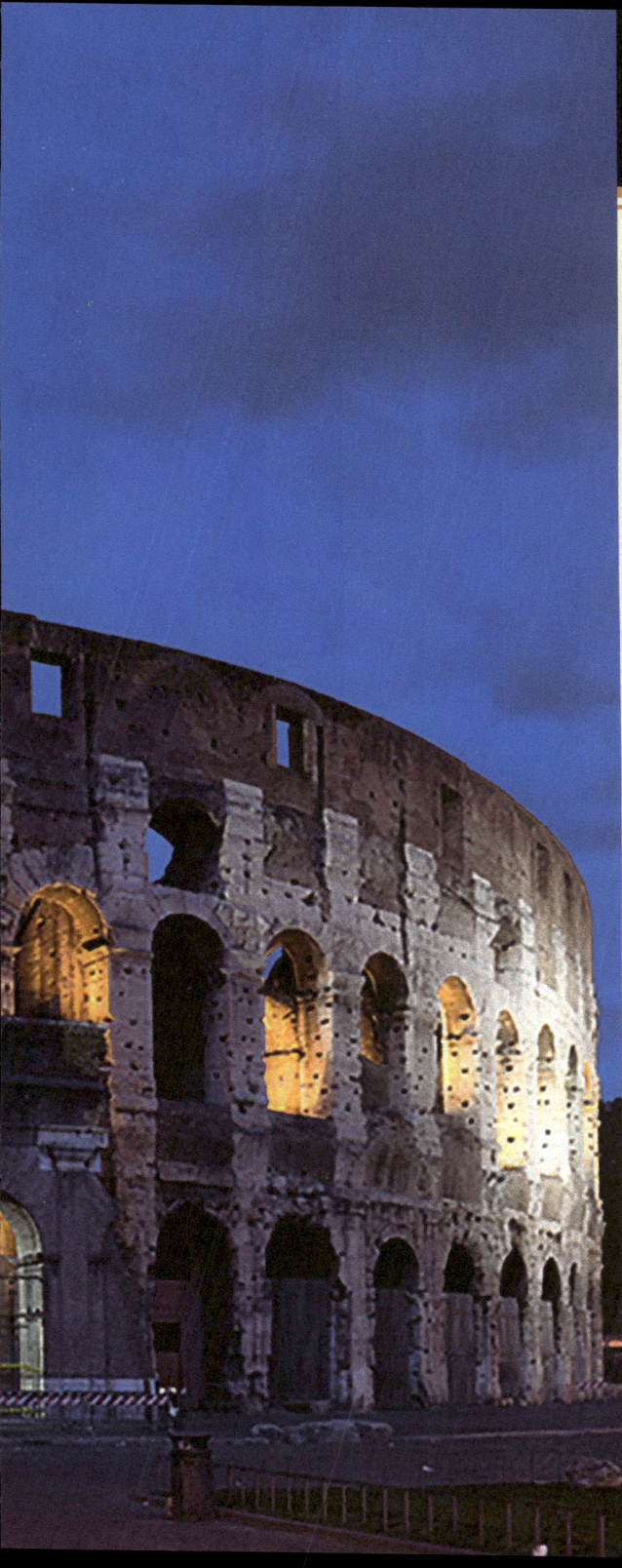

The largest amphitheater of the over 200 built throughout the Roman Empire, it was a standalone building. Its architecture displayed three levels of the classic Roman arches that were representative of the best of Ancient Roman design. The name Colosseum is thought to have come from Colossus of Rhodes, an ancient Greek statue that stood 108 feet tall.

The arches were used to keep the weight of the heavy stone to a minimum, yet keep the walls strong. The Colosseum had four different seating levels with tiered seats. Made of over a million tons of stone, bricks, and the Roman version of concrete, this amazing building is over 500 feet wide and over 600 feet long. It was also taller than the Colossus of Rhodes at 158 feet tall.

6782. P.Z. - ROMA. ESTERNO DEL COLOSSEO.

In addition to the fantastic structure that was built above ground there was a labyrinth of underground passages for the gladiators and animals so they could appear in and disappear from the arena's floor. There were 76 exits so that the thousands of people wouldn't trample each other when leaving the amphitheater. Despite earthquakes and the passage of thousands of years, a large portion of the building can still be seen today.

THE PANTHEON

The Pantheon was an enormous temple that was originally built for the Ancient Romans to worship their many gods and goddesses. The Pantheon had the largest unsupported dome worldwide for a period of over 1200 years. In the 1400s, the dome of the Florence Cathedral surpassed the size of the Pantheon's dome.

The dome is about 140 feet high and the same distance across its base, so it's a perfect sphere. To accommodate the weight at the top of the building, the Romans used lightweight volcanic rock. Sections of the Pantheon have been rebuilt over the centuries but it still stands as an icon of the incredible architecture produced by the Ancient Roman Empire.

STONE ROADS

The roads throughout Rome were of vital importance to their economy and also to their military. The Ancient Romans constructed a very advanced system of roads. Many of these roads are still in use today.

The saying "All roads lead to Rome" was certainly true during the time of the Ancient Roman Empire. By 200 AD, the Romans had designed and constructed over 50,000 miles of road from the city and throughout the vast area of the empire. Twenty-nine of the "highways" that they built led right to center of Rome.

The Roman military, called the Roman legion, was able to travel about 25 miles per day on these stone roads. The engineers of the roads held to strict guidelines during construction.

Stone Roads

The roads were built straight and also with the proper gradation to allow for water drainage so heavy rains wouldn't impede the military's progress. The roads had signs and mileage markers so that travelers could get their bearings.

The word "via" is the Latin for "road." Roman roads were generally named with the word "via," such as Via Appia, which simply means Appia Road.

AQUEDUCTS

Today in our modern homes we have toilets and underground sewage. Our cities have decorative fountains and when people want to relax they sometimes go to a spa. Surprisingly, the Romans enjoyed some of these same things in their civilization. They had public toilets and they also had sewage systems. They had beautiful ornate fountains with decorative statues.

They also had luxurious public baths with separate bathing areas for men and women. They went to these baths not only to bathe but also for entertainment, socializing, and healing. None of these innovations would have happened without the use of aqueducts to transport water along the pipelines and into the center of the city.

Aqueducts were structures that the Romans built specifically to carry water into the city. Many of these structures were constructed below ground. The water would flow into large public fountains. There, citizens would take their buckets to collect water and bring it to their dwellings. Over the years, the system became so sophisticated that wealthy citizens had running water in their homes.

The Romans didn't invent aqueducts. The Egyptian and Babylonian civilizations also had aqueducts. However, it was the Ancient Romans with their advanced engineering skills that greatly improved the construction of aqueducts.

They were really the first civilization that harnessed water's power for their purposes. Eventually, they built hundreds of aqueducts that could transport water from as far as 60 miles away.

Some aqueducts were built so well that they are still being used today. The famous Trevi Fountain in Rome gets its water from a version of one of Rome's original aqueducts, called the Aqua Virgo. There were so many aqueducts just in the city of Rome that if you added their lengths you would get a total of about 500 miles.

If you look at a photo of the aqueducts, you'll see that same stacking archway design that the Romans used on many different kinds of buildings. The Cloaca Maxima, part of Rome's original sewer system, is still in use today as part of the storm overflow water collection system. It's estimated that parts of this system are more than 2600 years old.

BRIDGES

In addition to aqueducts to carry water, the ancient Romans also built many stone bridges to transport people and vehicles over water. It's estimated that they built over 900 bridges throughout the empire. Many of these bridges are still standing today. As they did with their other structures, the Romans used arches to make their bridges strong and durable.

Built in 62 BC, the Pons Fabricius is the oldest bridge that still exists in Rome today. It was constructed across the Tiber with two large arches with a connecting arch between them. It's still used for pedestrians today.

Awesome!

Now you have learned more about Ancient Roman architecture and the buildings that are thousands of years old still standing today. You can find more Books about Ancient Roman history from Baby Professor by searching the website of your favorite book retailer.

Visit

BABY PROFESSOR
EDUCATION KIDS

www.BabyProfessorBooks.com

to download Free Baby Professor eBooks
and view our catalog of new and exciting
Children's Books

9 798869 410276